MWA1481306

The series 'Inner Light'

Book I. The Doctrine of Inner Light

Books by Konstantin Serebrov

Trilogy 'The mystical Labyrinth
in Russia':

1. The mystical Labyrinth in Russia
2. The mystical Underground of Moscow
3. On the Path of alchemical Fusion

The series 'Alchemical Teachings':

1. Practical alchemy
2. Spiritual Alchemy in Words and Pictures

The series 'Inner Light':

1. The Doctrine of inner Light
2. The Practice of Kriya-Yoga

The series 'Inner Christianity':

1. The Path of the Monk, part I
2. The Path of the Monk, part II
3. The 22 Mysteries of the Christian Way (together
with G. Gozalov)

The Doctrine of Inner Light

Konstantin Serebrov

Serebrov Boeken
The Hague

© Publishing House Serebrov Boeken, The Hague, 2006
Telephone/Fax: +31 (0) 70-352 15 65
E-mail: serebrovboeken@planet.nl
Website: www.thehermitagebookshop.com

English translation of a Russian manuscript 'Доктрина
внутреннего света' by Konstantin Serebrov, Moscow, 2001

'The Doctrine of inner Light'

ISBN13: 978-90-806321-1-0

Translator: G. Gozalov, The Hague
Editor: R. Winckel-Mellish, 'English Writers', Wassenaar
Design: W. Ross, Rossco Desctop Publishing, Amsterdam
and K. Serebrov, Moscow
The painting used for the cover: 'The Inner Light' by
E. Stepanova, Moscow.

The illustrations used in this book have been taken from
M. Maier's Symbola aurea mensae,
courtesy of Bibliotheca Philisophica Hermetica,
Amsterdam a.k.a. J.R. Ritman Library
Reprinted with the permission of the J. R. Library.

Contents

The Doctrine of Inner Light is a small philosophical and meditative work on the subject of the inner life. The author describes his search for inner freedom by means of meditation. We become acquainted with the fascinating inner travels in the invisible metaphysical worlds, the growing awareness of the radiant nature of the human soul and the practice of the accumulation of *inner gold*, which brings primordial youth and beauty back to the soul.

The book is illustrated with alchemical engravings, which represent all the stages of The Great Work up to its completion: the cultivation of the *alchemical garden*. These engravings might be the key to a deeper understanding of the meditations.

The reader will also find a supplement with the description of the breathing technique of concentration on the inner light and some other breathing techniques.

G. Gozalov
The Hague, July 2006

Once in one of my conscious dreams I met a Master, who initiated me into the doctrine of inner light. Immersed daily in my meditation, I refined the radiance of my essence through contact with the Spirit of the Master, who imparted the following knowledge:

'The idea of opening up the light origin of man will be the most important one of the third millennium. Every human being in the manifested universe is a radiant spark of the Absolute, Who installed His own divine nature in it and commanded His sons to return to His bosom, and to co-create in the universe together with Him. Everyone can open up his or her divine origin, hidden in the depth of the human soul. Moreover, when man cognises his inner nature, which is a radiant spark of the Absolute, he will be able to return to His Father's bosom, to the spiritual worlds of light, from which he has fallen into the manifested universe.

We are the sons of light, we are the sons of the sun. Hundreds of incarnations ago the Absolute charged the advanced human souls with the mission to descend into the manifested worlds and to elevate these to the worlds of radiant spirit. Millions of enlightened souls entered the darkness of the night, the pearl spheres of the manifested worlds, and scattered like leaves in the limitless Universe, the space of the invisible Spirit.

The sorrow of these souls who had to leave the divine worlds, mixed with the pain of existence on the millions of manifested planets, which accomplish the circles of life in the golden light of colourful suns. However, many of these souls - immersed in the illusory existence of the manifested Universe - forgot their divine nature.'

The Master taught me the basics of the breathing technique, which brings forth the inner light in man, and I practised what he had taught me.

After my practices, a radiant origin awoke in me, and this changed my entire life. During conscious dreaming I used to meet my mentor, who guided me on the path of light, refining my practices. Long after, he allowed me to transmit this knowledge to the world, to those who wish to evolve their inner light. The practice of inner light is a direct Path of ascension towards the divine nature of man. The theme of inner light appears in various spiritual traditions as well as in the main religions of the world. Saints in the Christian religion are represented on icons with a shining nimbus, which shows that they opened up their light origin as a result of constant prayer to our Lord Jesus Christ.

Buddhism says that he who experiences the highest nature of the mind as a void of radiant light, reaches enlightenment and liberation from the Wheel of Samsara.

Tibetan practices teach how to obtain the body of light and how to transit into a heavenly dwelling. The great teacher Padmasambhava in his treatise *Bardo Thodol*, known as *The Tibetan Book of the Dead*, tells about reaching liberation after death and transition into the radiant worlds. Namkhai Norbu, teaching the practice of Dzogchen, says that the ultimate purpose is to transform the physical body into a body of light and thus reach complete liberation.

According to Zen teachings the final goal of man who follows the Path, is the enlightenment of his inner nature and the attainment of immortality.

A spiritually developed human being feels that a radiant golden energy saturating every cell of their organism, while the soul harmoniously and naturally merges with the cosmos.

> *As long as the thoughts are obscured by ignorance*
> *The perishable body would still prevail*
> *It's however only the deception of the burdened feelings*
> *Where can I find my true 'Self'?*

Wang Wei

The theme of inner light is known in Sufi teachings as the path of a moth, which flies into the candlelight. Man, being incarnated, makes a journey of oblivion; he forgets his light nature. This is a journey away from God. Then, while in deep prayer, the unfading light of the most intimate state of unity illuminates his heart, and man who loves God, becomes aware of the pain of separation. It is not possible to realize the separation from God without realizing the unity with Him. The mystical path is paradoxical and there is no consequent proceeding from the state of separation from God to the state of unity with Him. This path is like a spiral and the opposites alternate.

In the beginning of the 19th century, the theosophical author Mabel Collins received a message from the higher spiritual hierarchies for the whole of humanity stressing the necessity to awaken man's light nature. She described this in her well-known book *Light on the Path*. The more man advances on the ascending Path to the divine worlds, the lighter becomes this thorny Path. Ultimately the blindfold falls off his eyes and unknown cosmic perspectives reveal themselves. Then man hears the heavenly call for unity with the Father, who gave birth to him.

The alchemist of the medieval ages aspired to find within himself the golden divine light, which he called 'the Inner Gold'. The efforts of the alchemist were directed towards transformation of the transient and egoistic personality of man into a truly spiritual being. The alchemical purification and elevation of man, which is a symbol for the path of initiation, has 7 stages. This is the path from darkness leading to the light, from ignorance to wisdom. The alchemist had to look into his soul in order to reach the very depth of his being. At the same time, he carried out some hidden mysterious work, in order to find within him the Philosopher's Stone.

The Philosopher's Stone was the great aim of the alchemist, who did everything he could to obtain it. This Stone can transform common metals into pure gold. It is a universal medicine against any disease, the elixir of life that can make man immortal. Due to the Stone man

obtains perfect happiness, and becomes an influential being in the
Universe, because through it he comes into contact with the Cause
of all Causes: the Absolute. A found Philosopher's Stone means in a
mystical sense, a completed transmutation of the lower animal nature of man into the highest divine nature. The culmination of this
'Secret Work' is the birth of a spiritually perfect man.

The Philosopher's Stone is the most perfect substance, shining
with golden light equal to that of the primordial matter of creation,
which came into being when the Fire of Divine Intelligence brought
cosmos into the original chaos.

Our radiant heavenly soul is a manifestation of the Philosopher's
Stone. The Art of Alchemy liberates her from the human body in
which she is imprisoned. Opus Magnum is the unity with God,
opening the path to immortality; the cognition of the way, enabling
the human being to develop divine qualities within itself.

This small work is dedicated to the theme of kindling the inner light
and achieving contact with our divine nature.

* * *

MEDITATIONS

It is possible for man to pursue the possession of wealth in the manifested worlds, but it is equally possible to dedicate one's life to the search of inner light.

Inner light is an inexhaustible source of bliss. The golden radiance of the soul is that very gem, of which seekers of truth have been in pursuit since immemorial times. Inner light comes from the depths of our essence. It penetrates into all secret recesses of the heart, blessing it with the highest grace. Inner light is that very wealth which is the foundation of our essence. Inner light flows from our Highest Self, thus illuminating the space of our soul.

When the human soul descends into the depths of the material worlds, she becomes saturated with the heavy breath of the manifested world and gradually loses her radiant quality. Then man feels overtaken by depression. If such a soul can immerse in her depths inner light will cure old wounds. The leaden heaviness within dissolves and a sensation of glaring purity of the heart rises instead. This light will illuminate man's way in the worlds hereafter.

Man's soul accumulates the particles of cosmic gold through meditation on the radiance of inner light. These remain with him until he spends them on outer life, but not even a scintilla of this cosmic gold can be bought for money. The only way to accumulate it is meditation upon the inner light. Inner light is the basic cosmic currency that has value in the worlds hereafter. We cannot take with us the wealth that we have gathered in the material worlds. No matter how persistently we strove for our millions of dollars, they always remain in the world of matter. We can take no material gain with us on our posthumous journey. Though this fact is annoying, it sobers us, reminding us of the necessity to acquire the inner gold, which stays with us after our death. Golden light born from inner peace is the cosmic currency, which has real value in other worlds, for it is an eternal gold, while objects of material luxury remain always in the relative world.

The cultivation of the inner gold is an infallible investment of our time and energy because we can take the results of our work with us into the world hereafter.

The source of inner gold is the eternal glory of the Absolute.

He is the Creator of the manifested worlds.

He has animated our souls.

He gave to us a particle of His imperishable glory.

Following His incessant call we can regain our lost inner wealth – our origin of light.

External wealth is not a bad thing, but it is not worthwhile as an ultimate goal. Many people chase only that kind of wealth, because they do not know anything about the life hereafter, they even fear the thought of it. For them the loss of the physical body means the loss of all they have gained during life. The theme of death amongst such people is often 'taboo' as a subject of discussion.

But if man honestly considers the reality in which he dwells, he realizes clearly that after death he will live in another, more subtle body. In those subtle worlds the only thing of value is the inner gold that we have accumulated in our souls. Inner light is the main source of the cosmic pollen, which through its volatility brings us to the highest worlds of light. If we do not wish to dwell in the dark and gloomy halls of the lower earthly astral plane after our death, we must pay heed, here and now.

If we are intelligent enough, we will take time to kindle our inner light, which is the source of inner well-being and happiness. If we radiate happiness, we attract positive outer circumstances, for inner wealth is always attractive. When you attain inner happiness, you will see how senseless the pursuing of outer well-being is, for your inner happiness will always be with you.

The radiance of inner light and the enchanting feeling of love can make you happy, and these cannot be bought with money or any material wealth. You can buy a good house, a car, create a comfortable situation for yourself, and even start to travel around the world. But, wherever you go, you will always be confronted with yourself. If there is no light in your soul, the outer world will just amuse you for a short while, without giving any true consolation.

But if you possess cosmic gold, then, wherever you are, whatever might happen to you, your soul is always ethereal and light, and you feel happy because you are always in contact with the source of bliss. With light in your soul, you will see how your heart opens itself to love, how it radiates its warmth to your neighbour. Moreover, you will receive a faithful love in return. Such a love cannot be acquired through money - dollars have no value for the inner light. Of course, we need means to live; as long as we carry a physical body we cannot live in the spirit alone. But it is advisable to maintain a sense of proportion always and everywhere.

Strive to gain inner gold during your earthly life – this is the way to cosmic wealth. Do not oppose outer wealth with an inner one; it is necessary to master both. Only then may we have a complete incarnation.

* * *

MORENIUS

The figure on the foreground on the left side represents a neophyte who is trying to study the theory and practice of obtaining the Philosopher's Stone alone, with only the help of books. The scene on the engraving symbolically shows that the neophyte, without the help of an experienced alchemist, is doomed to failure like the man, who, being unequipped, tries to climb over the vertical wall of the tower and will certainly find only his own death. The alchemist points to the earth, hinting to the neophyte, that the difference between the Materia Prima, out of which the Sulphur and the Quicksilver should be obtained, and the common earth, is a matter of principle.

Alchemical tradition has existed for several millenniums. An alchemist dedicates his entire life to the search of the Philosopher's Stone or the 'liquid gold'. Such a gold is also called 'the cosmic gold' and is capable of granting its owner immortality and an enlightened state, in which it is possible to cognise man's highest Self.

The frosty morning plunged me into the daily commotion. I got up quickly, trying to catch the rhythm of life and not waste time. At this moment I realized that I had completely identified with my body, and therefore my interest towards life had unfortunately become one-sided and pragmatic. Fragments of adventures I had caught in dreams were still in my mind, but I felt no inspiration in my soul.

I understood that the dream of maya caught me again in its net of limitation, and the joy in my soul faded. The problems and common programs had already invaded my consciousness. I almost forgot the main impulse of my life - the idea of liberation from illusions that my identification with the physical body casts on me. I had to do something quickly in order to rid myself of these alien influences. When I forget that I am a spiritual being, incarnated in a body for the purpose of self-realization, the dream of maya impresses on me its pragmatic programs, in which my soul finds neither joy nor inspiration.

Having decided to throw off the veil of earthly perception, I entered the inner recesses and sat down to meditate. The first minutes of my meditation were unsuccessful, sceptic thoughts roamed through my head, and a leaden heaviness swelled in my soul. But I didn't give up the will to change my perception. Gradually immersing in the depth I detached myself from heavy elements, and my soul felt extraordinary ethereal. I continuously asked a question, in deep silence: 'Who am I? Who am I? Who am I?' - until I could feel that I was not my body. I let my body relax and it became completely stiff. I experienced then clearly that I was untied from it.

I felt explicitly that my body is just a temporary garment, which is so perfectly included in my sphere of sensations that I do not see the difference between the garment and me. In order to remember it, I have to experience the sensation again and again, for identification with the body occurs instantly and insensibly. I have to enter another state of consciousness again and again to realize the difference between my body and me.

I started to immerse deeper within myself, until I came into contact with the energy of my Highest Self. It was a gentle impulse coming from my back. From that moment on I was aware of my spiritual task. The wind of the Highest Self filled me, and the light of my soul was kindled. I acquired inner strength. From now on I could live the day in harmony with my highest goals. I realized that if I could enter into the energy of my Highest Self every day, my life would become a real fulfilment of my higher task. I would acquire enough strength to accomplish my mission.

* * *

In order to change himself man should construct an inner alchemical laboratory, where the transformation of negative energy into the gold of the inner light takes place.

It is necessary to learn the technique of recreation of the inner light, which you can apply in your alchemical laboratory of conversion of the negative impulses, and the laboratory will begin to produce the inner light. This light fills the soul with pure bliss.

The process of inner transformation can be started, once the alchemical laboratory has been tuned up.

You should tune up the work of the laboratory in such a way that it elaborates the coarse part of your nature, transforming the psychological lead, which had piled up in your soul for many years, into gold. Certainly it will take quite a long time to accomplish the alchemical transformation. It will not be easy for you to tune up the work of the alchemical laboratory without the guidance of an experienced person who can restore the inner radiance of the soul and who can help you to flame up your own lamp and to feel its radiance.

There are many sorts of inner light, and it is not recommended that you radiate the cold light of the Snowy Queen.

This is a luciferic light and it materializes personality, which does not have an eternal life.

The cold radiance of the Snowy Queen is the light of the luciferic space that freezes the soul, and kills the essence. If man is filled with cold light, he cannot have joy with other people, with the blue sky and the light of the rising sun. That is why the Tradition recommends you start by searching for a person who has already kindled his own inner light, and who knows how to transform inner lead into gold. If you have not set your alchemical laboratory to work, you will always be in need of the outer warmth of your neighbour, a man or a woman.

MEDITATION 3

Learn to be aware of the silver light of your soul, and you will find inner freedom and purity. You have everything you need at your disposal: your own time, energy and an unbending intention.

* * *

AVICENNA

The engraving represents the first stage of the alchemical work. The Alchemists
smelt out of the Materia Prima the stable, dry and hot male principle, which is signi-
fied by the animal on earth, and the female principle, moist and volatile, represented
by the white bird which aspires to the vast space. The female principle is chained
to the stable male principle, for the purpose of preventing its evaporation and dis-
sipation in common life. There is a constant struggle between these two principles.
When an alchemist obtains in the Work the pure male principle out of Materia Prima, he begins to feel the eternal call of the spirit. This call is a lodestar illumining
one's Path, which lies through innumerable doubts and failures. Do not become des
perate, for the reflection of the eternal star always glistens before you.
If you manage to extract a pure female principle out of the Materia Prima, your soul
will aspire towards Anima Mundi. She will feel the breath of the eternal spring and
just for a moment may long for the unfathomable summits, which eternally attract
humanity. However the problem with the feminine Quicksilver is that it is too unsta-
ble to exist on its own. Inevitably it longs to fly away and to dissipate on the expanses

of life. That is why the stable male Sulphur continuously tries to embrace and hold the Quicksilver firmly.

Today the day began happier than yesterday, because this morning I realized that I am not the body in which I live on earth. I sat down to meditate, and soon immersed myself in my inner world, sensing a gentle vibration in the lower belly. At that moment I had become separated from my physical body, and realized that I am a subtle transparent being, whose shape is a precise copy of my physical body.

I was immersed in the world of metamorphoses, experiencing once more the moment when I was born, realizing clearly that birth on earth was death on the astral plane. I knew that I had to make a further step in my development during this incarnation on earth. I had a clear idea that I was born with a certain mission, and that I absolutely had to fulfil it. My further progress on the *golden ladder*, leading to the crests of the spirit, depended on it. But after some time I lost the thread of this awareness, and became identified again with my physical body. My consciousness woke up from time to time, and carried me away to my astral past, but the outer world pressed day-to-day reality upon me.

The subject of the astral worlds where people live before they incarnate on earth was outlawed in the land where I grew up. The reason was to prevent people from remembering that they are spiritual beings. I had to hide the fact that I remember myself, and that I know from which worlds I have incarnated on earth.

Now in meditation and approaching the Highest Self, I suddenly felt myself part of the great infinity encompassing the whole Universe. I entered a space, which was beyond the conceptions of reality that my mind could comprehend. There were no material objects, as I knew them on earth, and no familiar forms. There was only a resplendent infinity opening itself in the inner space of my soul. I never believed that I would ever leave the framework of material form, and enter the world of radiant void.

MEDITATION 4

My winged soul flew up to the indescribable heights of the radiant worlds, breaking away from the commotion of the manifested world in which she was incarnated. I realized that there is a great multiplicity of worlds, the beauty of which transcends the beauty of the earthly world.

* * *

The frosty morning met me with the first rays of sunshine, and my soul felt lighter. Today it was easy to meditate and immerse in myself. I concentrated on the perception that the material body is just a temporary garment that I shall have to leave behind.

I felt a sensation of ethereal euphoria and inner freedom when I realized that the physical body is just a door to the material world. Through my body I gain access into the worlds of matter. When I lose it, I immediately find myself in the astral world, which is as real as the material world, but seems ephemeral in comparison to it. My subtle body serves as the door to the astral world.

I made a personal discovery that there are two completely different worlds in which humanity exists: the physical and the astral. It is very difficult to become aware of both realities during the earthly life, because we lose our memory of the astral plane. People in general are firmly convinced that life on earth is the only reality, because we lose our memory of the past with every new incarnation. 'All this talk' about another world seems to us no more than a product of imagination. 'Otherwise,' we think, 'all people would remember astral life.' But the situation is different, and only few remember their life before incarnation. Isn't it easier for the majority to consider them madmen and daydreamers? Isn't that the simplest way?

Nevertheless, the memory of life in the worlds of matter is not wiped out by the loss of physical body. Those who die meet their friends and relatives who have passed earlier on the astral plane. They also remember their lives very well during incarnation. Once we learn to preserve our memory through the transition from the astral to the earthly world, we will remember all our incarnations.

And now the question arises: If we have two bodies that alternate, who are we really? Going deeper into meditation, you will receive an answer: 'We are the immortal beings; we change our bodies according to the worlds we inhabit.' Our immortal essence dresses her with various bodies, thus gaining access to all the worlds manifested by the Absolute.

As was already mentioned, the problem is that we lose our memory with the transition from the astral to the earthly world. That is why it seems as if we have our consciousness for the first time, although we still have many feelings and vague reminiscences, and these hidden sensations are preserved agelessly in our soul. But we are unable to pass the threshold of inhibition and gain access to our real memory. Some of us have succeeded to look into the depths of their memory, and they can clearly recall that they were incarnated on earth many times before.

Our mind tends to reject this idea, because it bows towards the material universe. The mind says: 'You can easily touch any object in the material world, but where is your astral universe? Can you touch or see it with your eyes?' With this the mind sets a sly trap for us, restricting our inner freedom. The perception of the physical body is only equipped to perceive the material universe, and not the astral one. This is the very reason for our blindness towards other worlds.

But still the question remains: What is the nature of our essence? You will find the answer in deep meditation. Our essence is a radiant spark of the Absolute, she is eternal and she is immortal.

Her destiny is to return into the bosom of her Father.

She must restore the lost connection with Him and find her divine origin again.

* * *

ROGER BACON

The alchemist in the monk's robe holds the scales in his left hand, where the fiery sulphur flames in the left cup, while in the right one liquid quicksilver boils. With the gesture of his right hand he hints at the subtle balance between the stable male principle, which aspires towards the spirit, and volatile female principle, which aspires to Anima Mundi, the Universal Soul. Only when there is a perfect balance and union between these two principles is the matter ready for the second stage of the alchemical Work.

The fiery Sulphur and the boiling Quicksilver are, however, not able to find reconciliation; they are in a state of war. As a result of continual fighting, they forget about the highest purpose of their birth: the aspiration towards the highest worlds and further transmutation needed for this. The war exhausts them and makes them powerless. The female principle is according to its volatile nature, almost completely unable to coexist with the stable male principle. It is too limiting for the female principle to exist together with something which cannot fly to the heights. The male principle in its turn cannot grow and become transformed without the female principle, and that is their dilemma and good fortune at the same time.

It is necessary to find the third substance – the Salt, which is able to reconcile these two parties fighting to death.

Every morning I was confronted with the same problem: how can I cognise my own essence? The first minutes of today's meditation were not really successful, because I was trying to get rid of the chaos that piled up in my soul while I was travelling in subtle worlds in my dream body. The journey in other dimensions was the extension of earthly life, and did not bring me any closer to the gates of essence. On the earth I meet people in the streets of the city, and in my dreams I meet them there in the dream body. But the very core of these encounters remained all in the same shallow key.

I vainly thought that people in the worlds hereafter became more refined than on earth. Deep disappointment awaited me. Man remains himself anywhere, and if he did not wake up for the life of the Spirit on earth, he remains as ignorant in the other worlds as he was on earth. One thing was clear; I had to look either on earth or beyond its borders for a man who had reached his divine source. The presence of such a person is indispensable; the light of the soul will not turn into fire without him.

I ask the Master:

'What is my essence?'

He answers:

'You yourself are this mysterious essence. If you want to feel it, then immerse yourself in the peace of your own heart every morning. However if you identify with your body, then the words, 'remember yourself,' lose their meaning, and turn into a mental scheme, residing in your head.'

'The trouble with mental schemes is that they do not bring a real living sensation. They may excite you for a while, but your day-to-day perception will bring everything back to where it was.'

'When in your morning meditation you perceive your body standing apart, then the words 'remember yourself,' will remind you, that you are an incarnated spirit,' he went on. 'If you have realized this, try to see how the machinery of identification and de-identification with the body works,' he concluded.

Life limited by the restrictions of the body does not satisfy me. I remember the inner freedom, which carries me away to the crests of the spirit. Opening up my essence I feel pieces of golden light which arise from the depth of my soul. Without this light my life becomes a depressing existence.

Is there any difference between the two concepts of my soul and my essence? Most probably, these words describe one and the same phenomenon, but from different angles. There is an answer to the question: 'How can I open up my essence?'

'Meditate daily on her primordial light.'

The light of the soul is the base of success in both inner and outer worlds. It attracts the outer well-being, gives strength to reach one's goal, sustains the state of inner balance and happiness.

The golden light which shines in our soul, saves us from life's problems, and is a promise of mysterious happiness. Could man ever renounce the victory over himself?

* * *

The sunny morning met me joyfully and affably. I admired the beauty of the frosty sky and immersed myself in meditation. The immersion in myself started smoothly and insensibly, I wanted to de-identify with the body and perceive myself as an incarnated spirit, in order to realize my destiny.

I gradually get the notion that I am able to exist in two worlds: the material and the astral. Nevertheless, dwelling in the physical world, I vaguely perceive the astral one, and meditation is the best means of recollection.

In the deep meditation my essence fills up with golden radiance, and I clearly realize that I am a spark of the Absolute. I need to unite with my Father, to feel the unity and the limitless closeness.

My radiant Highest Self is the only source of inspiration for me in the infinity of the manifested worlds.

Liberated from the imprisonment of matter I enjoy feeling myself a spiritual being.

I discover regretfully that in the astral world I identify very much with the astral body, so that I grow apart even more from the golden radiance of the soul. And again intriguing transformations blind my mind, alienating it from my essence. I forget my essence again; I do not remember her radiant face anymore.

After the extensive investigations I begin to realize that the astral world is the same prison for the radiant essence as the physical world is. It has only more dimensions of freedom. I become convinced that to feel passion for the astral worlds draws me away from inner freedom as much as investigation of the manifested worlds.

Going deeper in myself, I discover that my radiant essence dwells in the celestial world, and appears in the relative worlds dressed in different shells. These shells might be material, ethereal as well as astral. Wherever, in whatever cosmos I have been incarnated, a body, my present point of support, always entrapped me.

It is a pity that the human essence, whatever garments she puts on, gradually becomes identified with them. Each body is just a point of support in one world or another, and however beautiful and diverse these are, a man dwelling there will always be far away from the Absolute.

Dwelling in the relative worlds, I can rarely hear the voice of my Father; it happens only when I immerse in deep meditation.

Perceiving myself as an inextinguishable spark of the Everlasting One, I can return to my heavenly Father when I would rise from ashes . Dwelling in any of the manifested worlds, I can hear His breath when I immerse in myself.

I have an opportunity to restore connection with the Absolute, which was lost long ago, because I am His radiant spark. Though, in the relative worlds this link is hardly discernible. How sad, that the voice of the Absolute is almost unheard in the abyss of the forgotten worlds. But still it is possible to discover the tie with Him being immersed in the radiance of one's own soul.

 As soon as I forget the golden radiance of my essence, being identified with one of the bodies of my soul, I am imprisoned by the glamour of the world in which I happen to be.

Having acquired control over my subtle bodies I will be able to penetrate the endless worlds of the manifested universe. But still I need to remember myself as an immortal radiant Spirit.

For me it is most important to perpetuate an invisible link with the Absolute, who gave birth to all of us, and not be lost amongst the great diversity of the manifested worlds, forgotten by Him in of one of my bodies.

Remember that you are an eternal radiant spark of the Absolute; do not forget your divine nature.

Remember that the everlasting light of your Father is in you.

Remember, that nothing and nobody can substitute the bliss that awaits you in His radiance.

* * *

It was morning again and my eyes reflected the light of the pale yellow sun.

Again I conceived a wish to immerse in the unknown depths of my Self. I am pleased to know that I am not my physical body, for I can leave it in the ethereal body when I wander in other dimensions.

In this meditation I enjoy leaving the physical body and being freed from it. I watch the metamorphoses of my logical mind with pleasure and see how all earthly aims and programs hopelessly collapse, turning to dust and ashes, becoming unreal. They are of use only when I am completely in love with the material puppet of perpetual delusion.

If I know that I am not my body, its programs cannot be set as a goal, because it is just a temporary shelter for the soul to incarnate. Who am I then, if I am not my body? Who sent me to this planet? Is there a truthful purpose for this incarnation?

If I am a spirit, then the patrimonial programs are as strange to me as the fallen leaves.

Did I incarnate in order to cognise my soul, to unearth the mystery of myself? I wish to spend all my life looking for the key to the mystery of the Egyptian sphinx.

The goals of people who identify with their body cannot be my reference points.

People around me are sleeping within themselves, being immersed in the hypnosis of incarnation. They are unable to realize that they are not their bodies of incarnation.

When I wake up from the worldly hypnosis I realize that it is hopelessly absurd to imitate the sleeping people.

I won't regret that I spent my entire life recollecting who I am and from where I came. I do not spare the time awakening from the dream of maya, though I know that only a few succeed in doing it.

The world is beautiful if I realize that I have received this body temporarily in order to find the key to myself. The world is beautiful when I am aware of the fact that I am something else besides my body and when I constantly try to unveil this magic mystery.

Who am I and where will my path lead me?

I get accustomed to the fact that in the process of gaining self-knowledge I easily leave the body and return into it.

I realize suddenly that the world of incarnated human beings is not my final stop.

I slept long in my body, but all at once I woke up.

Being outside the body I see that it has stiffened into a strange posture, and realize suddenly that the body is just the means of cognising the inner freedom.

One can dedicate one's entire life achieving it.

I see that the world consists of moving waxworks, which harden immediately when the spirit leaves them.

I see that it is senseless for me to strive for outer comfort, for I can find it within.

I begin to see the play of the illusory world, and to find my ways in the space of its laws.

I leave my body, however, every night, piercing the world behind the mirror, and in the morning I put on my body again.

And though my mind tries to persuade me of the contrary, I learn to avoid the traps it sets.

* * *

ARNOLD DE VILLA NOVA

The wise alchemist with the grey bear, dressed in dark garments, points out with his left hand to the ceremony of the alchemical wedding between the Red King and the White Queen, the union between the pure male principle aspired to the spirit and pure female principle aspired to Anima Mundi. This union is necessary to prevent the volatile female element being dissipated in the common life. The male principle needs this union because otherwise it is not capable of further transformation. The golden ring, the symbol of their marriage, represents the principle of the Salt, the hidden element which binds them.

If the Red King, pure Sulphur, will not mate with the White Queen, the pure Quicksilver, they will never be able to realize themselves as the particles of the Divine Origin of All Origins. They will then be doomed to roam eternally in the abyss of delusion in the fallen worlds of the manifested universe. Only when they unite their efforts in their aspiration to the highest worlds, will they be able to cognise the mystery of the Universe, which is hidden from the earthly eye by the veil of ignorance. In order to reach the invisible heights on the thorny Path of Reintegration, the Red King has to become one with the White Queen.

MEDITATION 9: THE GOLDEN RADIANCE OF THE SOUL

Today I spent the first minutes of meditation recovering from the chaos and feelings of senselessness in my soul.

My mind is filled with various concerns, fragments of yesterday's experiences and recollections of dreams.

Sometimes in dream I lose the intensity of the radiance of the soul and descend into chaotic spheres. I recollect some dreams filled with encounters with strange people on the astral plane, and this only exhausts me, dragging me to the very surface of myself. Therefore it is necessary to detach myself from my dreams, for then I identify with my subtle body.

After 10 minutes of meditation the chaotic gliding on the surface of my mind stops, and I begin to immerse in the inner world, pondering upon the golden light, which arises from the depths of my nature. At first the mind judges these thoughts as absurd, but I persistently break through its scepticism, overcoming the invisible resistance. Putting a stop to the ceaseless flow of thoughts, I immerse in silence constantly reciting: 'I am the light of inner bliss,' until the light begins to shine within my soul. Inner light purifies me, renewing my inner world, which by the end of the day is filled with mundane commotion and problems. I realize that if I want to keep the light of my soul, I have to restore her radiance every day.

If I do not, the outer world soon wipes away her beauty and heavenly charm.

Due to meditation I begin to see how the mind instantly merges with the object towards which its attention is directed.

If my mind directs its attention to the outer world and its problems, I also go down with it to the bottom of the endless difficulties and my consciousness loses its lustre.

Immersing in daily meditation, I concentrate my mind on inner light. The soul, plunging into its radiance, becomes as clear and pure as rock crystal. During the day I try to remember that I am in essence the gentle light that flows out of my soul. As long as I hold on to it, I am in a state of balance and inner peace. But immediately when I become involved in one problem or another I forget that I am a luminous being, filled with beauty and magic charm.

Immersing in the golden radiance, I feel never-fading joy and realize that the body is just a temporary refuge for the wandering spirit. A sensation of enchantment comes over me, an understanding that I live in a magic world created by the Absolute. I contemplate with wonder how the world is animated by the immortal souls entering physical bodies, and leaving them when the time comes. I feel sorrow that at the moment of incarnation they forget that they are spiritual beings, and think that they are the material shells in which they incarnate. This world of charm is as beautiful as it is treacherous, because it casts a sweet dream of illusion. The illusion is that incarnated man identifies with the transient body and forgets his spiritual nature, his Divine origin.

We are the spiritual children of the Absolute and the memory of it gives us the power to return to His radiant palace.

It is not necessary to leave this world, or to immerse in a hermit's life in order to experience the state when you perceive the radiance of the inner light. You only need to sit down in meditation and feel the golden light in the depth of your soul. Then life will be filled with the breath of eternity.

What can be more beautiful than an inexhaustible source of light filled with inner grace?

It is possible to reach your Divine origin by intensifying the radiance of the essence.

It is impossible, however, to open up your Divine nature, to recall your higher destiny while being identified with the body

The mind deceives us continuously by telling us: 'There are no higher worlds, because you cannot see them.' In order to look into another world, open your inner eye; in order to recall your divine nature, touch upon your Highest Self.

Remember your Self, remember that you are a divine spark of the Absolute.

Don't fall into the traps of the mind, be careful with your physical perception and remember that it is meant only for the material world.

* * *

In today's meditation I immersed myself easily and smoothly in the golden radiance, experiencing clearly that I am this very light, an inextinguishable spark of the Absolute Origin of all Origins.

When my mind is fixed on the inner light, I perceive myself as the light, which makes the world of my personality collapse like a house of cards. The world of my personality is based only on the perception of myself as a transient body.

My soul has accumulated resentments and claims towards the world, and towards people whom I did not let into my heart. In order to clear this, I bring the inner radiance to certain intensity and direct the light to the dark areas of the soul. If the reservoir of light substance is big enough, it dissipates the dark spot and the soul restores her radiance.

In this manner I restore step by step the radiance of those parts in my soul which are filled with grief, envy and resentment. Exploring my inner world, I become convinced that any negative feeling entering the soul creates a dark spot there.

Directing inner light to it, I liberate my soul from the heaviness of the negative emotions. But the light of my essence becomes dim, and I need to restore its radiance again.

Having made a list of relationships which left dark spots in my soul, I direct the light substance to these spots.

The inner light restores the golden radiance of the soul, releasing her from negativity.

Life's problems waste the light of the human essence and she fades away, burdened with a leaden heaviness which gradually chokes the inner life.

Ordinary life takes away the radiance of the soul, imprisoning her in a greyish room without joy, where there is neither interest for life nor fineness of perception.

The state of ill feeling darkens the light of the soul. If the resentment has infiltrated the heart, it creates a dark spot on its radiance. Jealousy creates deep dark stripes in the soul and the radiance of the soul is lost for a long time.

Envy darkens the inner light.

Revenge and malevolence are deadly for the inner radiance. Never cherish them in your soul.

Irritability corrodes and empties the soul.

Spilling of sexual energy darkens the soul.

Even the slightest negative feeling weakens the radiance of the soul, leaving a dark spot on the ethereal body.

Man, incarnated on Earth carries within his soul a sacred potential of light, which is too often spoiled during life and as a result the soul loses her original radiance and darkens.

The practice of opening up of the inner light restores the lost radiance and an extraordinary ethereality and romanticism return to the heart.

It is indispensable for the opening up of the inner light to keep a minimal reserve of the subtle energy with which it is possible to kindle the inner fire. Immersed in the inner radiance man begins to realize that he is this very light and nobody is able to take it away from him.

If I am an immortal light then it is not worthwhile to envy other people, because all joy is within me.

If I am a primordial light then it is not worthwhile to feel offended by other people, because they are not yet aware of their own radiant origin.

If I am the light then there is no need to hunt for external happiness, because my happiness is within me.

Accumulating the inner radiance I attract the elusive fortune.

If I am the silver light, then there is no reason to feel irritated by other people.

If I am the golden light, I have no reason to oppress others, demanding their obedience.

MEDITATION 10

If I am the conscious light, then there is no need to feel jealous, because all the love is within me.

* * *

The meditation began by the realization that I am a spiritual being, who can easily leave his body to travel to other dimensions.

I recollected that I have incarnated hundreds of times on the planets of our Universe, covering my Self with many different bodies, carrying various images. I just have to recall myself, to recollect who I am and restore the lost memory.

The second step was to kindle the inner light, concentrating on the middle of my chest, and gradually the radiant space flames up within me. When the radiance of light has intensified, I direct it to the darkened spots of my soul, which were caused by events of the past. I illuminate them with inner light, trying to dispel the gloom, which has settled in my soul through many years.

The inner light quickly dissipates fears and ill feelings that have become like asphalt banks in the depth of the left side of my body.

Having directed light to the frowsy cellars of my soul, I watch how the dark protuberances of suppressed negativity break out. Once rid of them, I feel extraordinarily relieved. I concentrate on inner light, which shines more intensively with every moment, dissipating the traces of the karma of my faults.

When the perception goes down to the level of the instinctive centre, the heavy energy on the animal level is emitted into the atmosphere. The inner light elevates me, placing the point of perception on the level of the heart, granting me an opportunity to be in a refined state all day long. From that moment on I feel lighter and more romantic, life for me is no longer prosaic and monotonous.

The inner light purifies the darkened parts of the soul, wiping off personal history by restoring the radiance of the essence.

The applying of the technique of inner light easily restores the radiance of the ethereal body. It is the inner light which thrusts forward darkness from the soul, liberating her from the consequences of heavy karma. All my heaviness has piled up in the left side of the body, concentrated in the form of psychological lead. It is not visible, but it constantly radiates heavy emanations into the atmosphere around me. Purifying myself from these banks of lead, I feel ethereal and volatile, and my eyes feel more warm and sincere. I feel the same radiance of the soul and an extraordinary feeling of love towards the world around me, which I used to feel in my early childhood.

When the identification with the physical body disappears, the feeling of inner freedom rises in the soul. Flying on the wings of inner light, man can reach immensely distant prospects and enjoy the perception of other worlds.

Inner light releases the mind of old unwanted refuse and prepares it to perceive sacred ideas streaming from the Spirit of Time. The flow of life is unnoticeable and its changes are elusive. It is necessary to enter the new pattern of its beauty and to be open to the new wind and to new possibilities.

But if soul and mind are swamped by memories of the past, then new things can never penetrate through the barricade of thoughts and passions. The inner light cleans the mind and heals the soul from the wounds of the past. Our past with all its experiences is like a used-up ore, which serves no purpose. It is possible of course to be constantly busy in the mind, remembering the same experiences, but it is better to enjoy fresh moments of life. Man's personal history, nevertheless, stands in the way. Inner light wipes off the personal history, preparing the space of the soul for new experiences.

* * *

MARIAM: THE QUINTESSENCE OF THE SULPHUR AND QUICKSILVER

A woman-alchemist in long garments points to the stony hill, which symbolizes the Materia Prima. This is obtained by means of transmutation the pure Sulphur – the upper Vessel, and pure Quicksilver – the bottom vessel. The two currents between these two vessels – the purifying ascending current and the coagulating descending current, indicate the process of the alchemical Work. It should result in the Quintessence of the Sulphur and Quicksilver – the plant with five blossoming buds, which symbolizes the appearing of the matter Rebis.

If the volatile Quicksilver chooses for the secret union with the fiery Sulphur, and if the Red King chooses for the alchemical marriage with the White Queen, then a possibility will arise for them to create under the cloud of night, the third principle, which has the qualities of both parental principles. This marvellous plant will blossom with white flowers, which will long for the inner sun. They will open their petals to its radiance and will become filled with eternal beauty and heavenly fragrance.

The Red King will fasten his eye to the heavens, and the White Queen will look at the rising moon covered with the silver mist, and they will again find their heavenly primogeniture.

Being immersed in meditation early in the morning I realized, that the gold of inner light is the sacred centre of the human being, while the body is a separate entity. I look at my body from aside and see that it is not me but some strange person, answering to my name. He has been misguiding me for so many years, stating that I am him, while he is me.

I say to him:

'I perceive myself as an immortal spirit, while you are my outer, corporal cover. When your time is over, and the flesh smoulders to ashes, I shall again return to the radiant world, which is invisible to you. Between us there will always be a struggle without rules.'

The flesh tells me:

'Identify forever with me, and forget about the subtle world, the memory of it is of no use on earth.'

I wanted to take this perishable flesh with me into the subtle world, but the flesh got stuck in the material world like the proverbial camel in the eye of the needle.

The perception of the flesh is limited by the world of matter. When I manage to separate myself from it, realizing that I am a radiant spirit, I come into the worlds of golden radiance.

'These worlds are incomprehensible to you, my transient flesh. Though you try to drag me down to earth and mislead me, I still manage to steal my way into the world of Spirit through an invisible door. I have to live the life of my essence and not that of a material puppet. I am so fluent, that I cannot be myself; I change my outlines and forms like water. My fluidity enables me to be what you are, my perishable flesh, and if I forget about this transformation, I begin to live my life as if I am you.'

I forget my longings, being identified with my body, which is full of concern, and receive in return things that belong to it.

The task of a luminous being is to restore his lost memory about himself, because this is lost with every new incarnation, so that we forget the history of our past incarnations in the manifested universe.

Try to immerse in yourself. To do this take a seat in a posture convenient for meditation, straighten your spine and relax the muscles. Stop the turmoil of your thoughts and concentrate on the point in the middle of your chest. You will feel, that inner peace sets in after a while, and you will hear the distant voice of your essence.

Do not pay attention to the atmosphere of the room, or the house, or the street, which exists apart from you and constantly distracts you. Listen attentively to the voice of your Self, the voice of your essence.

The next stage comes when you learn to kindle the inner light by means of a special technique - you can learn this technique in the Hermetic School. Then you will be able to immerse into its radiance, purifying your soul from the problems and dark spots, which extinguish your inner radiance.

The next stage comes when you learn to shift at will the point of your perception. This is also a special technique, which is taught practically in the School.

When guided by the Master you will succeed to consciously change your perception, you will begin to notice the illusory nature of this world.

Then you will be able to investigate your own depths, and make wonderful discoveries.

You will learn to distinguish the sensations of the physical body from those of the ethereal and astral bodies. You will also be able to distinguish the sensations of your essence from emotions, which were cast over you by your current selves.

Having lost the sensation of the physical body, you will begin to perceive the ethereal body, and then afterwards the essence, and then you will discover that the mind still holds on to scepticism, in this way misleading us. Then you will remember death and the necessity to transit to another world.

The day will come when you will realize that your mind has been deceiving you during your entire life. Then, stepping aside from the body, you will see with amazement that it lies there immobile, while you float above it. All your sensations, however, have remained the same. You only got rid of your flesh – your point of support in the manifested world – and you proceed with your life in your new body.

Immediately other problems and perspectives emerge.

But if we believe the deceptions of our mind and have failed to develop a subtle perception during our life, then we will keep this delusion even in the subtle worlds.

And when we have memories of previous incarnations, we shall be surprised to discover that our delusion repeats itself again and again.

We incarnate on earth and live the life of our physical point of support, taking it for ourselves. And when it dies, we enter the world hereafter again with our mystery remained unveiled.

Oh what poor little souls we are. We fall asleep and dream that we are of flesh and blood. How incredibly wrong we are!

* * *

When I woke up it was already noon, and people walked merrily in the street. Though it was no longer early morning, I decided to immerse myself in meditation and in doing this realized, that I was completely identified with the flesh – the point of support in matter. My first task is to detach myself from it and to feel the taste of inner freedom. Therefore, starting to meditate I wait until the five senses of the physical body become still. These are hearing, taste, smell, sight and touch. When they are still, I am sure that I have become separated from the influences of my physical point of support.

The next task is to quieten my astral point of support, which is always overwhelmed by emotions related to my personal history. If I can manage to quieten my emotions, this will mean that I am detached from the perception of my astral point of support. Only then I am disconnected from my personal structure, from all my current 'selves'.

The next task is to set the mind at rest. When that is done, one can be sure that one is detached from his or her points of support in the manifested worlds.

By then I am face to face with myself, with my essence. In this phase it is important not to identify with the atmosphere of the place where I meditate. Identifying with the external atmosphere is a trap in which I can fall allowing me to miss my goal.

The next stage is to experience the void, the empty space within me, the so-called 'silent void' where there is nothing. I enter an empty range of perception, which is the transitional moment before perceiving the true essence. I have to pass through the sensation of the emptiness in my heart, the emptiness in my soul.

The next moment in meditation is the opening up of the essence. If I proceed successfully, then the silver light will gradually start to shine within me and it will fill the entire space of the soul with a feeling of incredible purity. I note that crossing the space of emptiness is an important event, which opens up the essence.

From this moment on I am able to consciously control my perception. I may flame up the inner light, but I may also direct my attention to the shifting of my perception. I can shift my point of perception to a certain place outside the body close by the middle of the neck, and experience de-identification with the flesh. Now it becomes obvious, that the physical body is only a material puppet and I feel amazed that the mind could deceive me so long, keeping me in total delusion.

Continuing to immerse within, I reach the level of super-conscious perception, where I feel the radiance of my Highest Self, the true freedom, a freedom I have never felt before.

This freedom is related to the highest worlds and I feel how the drop of my personality dissolves in the ocean of creation. But at the same time I do not lose the sensation of my Self, on the contrary it becomes even brighter and stronger.

I am no longer limited to my outer points of support in the manifested worlds, I have crossed the border of the fallen world, I have become free, I have returned to myself – to that Self, which eternally soars in unattainable spiritual height.

Now I can experience my closeness to the Absolute, closeness to the Father who has created me. I can experience the truth of my being. I am part of Him, I am His Divine Spark.

The inner light flows gradually through my whole being. I perceive myself as a Russian Matryoshka, made up of several points of support, the one inserted in the other. This is the very core of illusion. I take myself, the spiritual being, as my bodily points of support in other worlds.

My Highest Self is concealed under the cover of eight physical points of support, eight seals, and it is not easy to find it.

It is like a precious pearl locked in nacre, resting on the bottom of the ocean.

I want to find this nacre, which contains the radiant sun of my Highest Self.

I become a hunter of jewels, hidden in the depths of my soul. In my daily meditations I look for the nacre, in which the precious pearl of radiant freedom is hidden.

I become a pearl diver. I am the hunter of inner changes. I try to penetrate into the depths where my blinding essence dwells.

I try to flow together with golden radiance, in order to feel the unity with my Father, to dive into the reality of cosmic life, to get out of the shell in which I am imprisoned, and to meet the brilliant splendour of the cosmos face to face.

Having tasted this freedom, I can no longer remain in the prison of physical perception, the languorous cell of my body is too narrow for me, I am tired of being a snail, carrying my own box.

I wish to become a butterfly, a radiant being, which disappears from this reality and becomes transformed into golden light.

Sometimes I feel a powerful wave of light, which can absorb me forever. But I know that I will always be able to return to this world. I know that the highest light will not dissolve my individuality, but will only lead me to myself.

In our inner nature we are luminous beings which do not have a certain form, or a fixed abode. We dwell as golden light in the highest worlds and only the laws of the fallen world force us to manifest in visible forms, to be one person or another.

But when I reach final liberation and become a pure primordial light, then I shall dwell beyond the limits of the world of forms, without losing the opportunity to incarnate. I am a radiant light, I am a particle of primordial light of the Absolute. I shine in the darkness like an invisible inextinguishable sun. The primordial light of the Highest Self purifies the points of support in which it enters.

When I come in contact with the silver light, inspiration fills my heart and I aspire towards the Absolute Origin of all Origins.

* * *

MEDITATION 14: THE SUBJECTIVITY OF THE PERCEPTION OF THE AS-
TRAL WORLD

I was always preoccupied with the question of whether I will be
able to develop myself further in the world hereafter?
There are eight spheres of life there, which means that I shall be in
one of them.
The first three spheres can be conventionally united and called hell,
and those with heavy karma go there; the fourth sphere serves as a
purgatory as well as the intermediary state between incarnations.
There are four higher spheres in which people with light karma go
as well as those who are striving for self-knowledge.
There is, however, an incorrect opinion that if a person has not been
concerned with self-cognising during his life, he will certainly do so
after his death.
This sounds rather improbable, because man after his death comes
into a subjective space of consciousness, which he has created during his lifetime.
There exists in the world hereafter, side by side with the objective
reality containing the prototype of earthly world, a subjective reality, which is built by each person individually. Every human being
there lives at least in two realities, subjective and objective. The difference between the magician and the common person is that the
magician can create a world in which he can invite other persons to
be with him.
The subjective world of the common person is a monotonous selec-
tion of social clichés from which he himself tries to run away. There
is a minimum of romanticism and no flights of the soul into heights
beyond the boundaries, neither God nor His angels are there. This
kind of subjective world is empty and doomed. The common person spends millenniums on earth and in the astral spheres situated
near it, without making any attempt to climb the ladder of spiritual
ascension. He is motionless in his ignorance, he is impersonal and

one-track minded, he is blindfolded and cannot see the light of Divine reality. Such a person remains beyond the path leading to the highest worlds, the highest astral Schools. It is not that he is not admitted there, he just doesn't notice them. He is blind in the world hereafter to the same extent as he was on earth, for his ignorance follows him everywhere.

The point is that man's personality does not disappear after the death of his physical body, on the contrary, the number of his current 'selves' can even grow. Those who try to observe their various selves during their life on earth, will have that opportunity in the world hereafter. Moreover a man, who strove to cognize the nature of his soul, will gain great opportunities and advantages there.

Those who did not strive to cognise themselves on earth, will also not be able to do so in the world hereafter.

If in the physical world the physical body was a serious obstacle for cognising man's spiritual nature, then in the world hereafter the same obstacle will be the astral body. For it has the same negative and positive aspect as the physical one. If you master travel in the dreams by power of intention, then you will, with the same ease travel in the worlds hereafter. In this way you will have an opportunity to come down to the lower spheres to visit those who live there, but they will not be able to penetrate into the higher spheres because their heavy karma will not allow them to do so.

There are in the world hereafter realms related to the world's religions: Christianity, Buddhism, Hinduism, and also the worlds of magic realities. One can travel infinitely in these worlds, cognising the creations of man.

Every man will find in the world hereafter those things that he believed in, and things he was longing for during his life on earth.

If man does not strive to cognise his radiant nature as a spiritual particle of the Absolute, he will wander in the worlds hereafter just as he did on earth, restricted by his own perception. If he did not strive to cognise his Divine individuality, he is doomed to infinite wandering.

For our life on earth as well as in the world hereafter is determined by our perception.

Being engaged in the exploration of our inner worlds, we have a chance to become members of the highest astral Orders, in which advanced humanity lives and continues to work along the path of reintegration, the path of ascension towards the Absolute. But if man during his lifetime begrudges dedicating all his resources, time and money to the investigation of these matters, he will get into a losing situation in the worlds hereafter, compared to those who did otherwise.

Now it is necessary to solve the important problem of how to keep contact after death with the Master and the inner School. Tradition states that the best guarantee for meeting in the worlds hereafter is to continue the work of building the inner School which was started during life on earth.

* * *

RAIMOND LULLI

The matter Rebis – the child born out of the marriage of the Red King and White Queen, needs constant protection from both the male and female principles. They will later take care of the development of the child. The Rebis consists of a new substance, pure Sulphur and pure Quicksilver, which are fused in equal proportion. This substance contains higher qualities than the parental principles. Nevertheless it is unequipped to sustain life, and needs constant care and preparation for further transformations. The alchemist points to the guardians of the child, whose function is to prevent the matter Rebis from being completely dissipated in life. His left hand rests on the hilt of the sword, indicating that the matter Rebis needs the secret fire for further transmutation.

The delicate child of the Red King and White Queen needs constant care before he becomes a heavenly androgen. This innocent infant germinated by the fiery Sulphur and the moist Quicksilver does not have a stronghold in life, he soars in the world hereafter and does not dare to step on the sinful earth. The world is strange for him, and he therefore needs the protection of the wise Alchemist, who has lavished the attentions of the stable male principle and the volatile female on the child.

Once I moved to a new place, abandoning a place with an ideal atmosphere perfectly suited for meditations.

After several days in the new place I felt a dreary solitude and separation from the impulse of the School.

I decided to find out what the cause of my state was, and, immersed in meditation, I discovered that the house in which I lived was enveloped between two dense energetic shells. These shells created a heavy atmosphere without space for inner development, and did not allow me to connect with the subtle worlds.

The inner light was fading, I found myself in the locked room, without contact with the Ray. I had an acute feeling of the senselessness of my existence, and I even conceived a wish to stop my life.

Despite the inner despair I managed to break through these shells and restore the lost contact with the Master, and then, through him, I restored contact with the Ray itself, so that the golden light started to shine in my soul again.

I gained access to the inspiration of the Ray again and realized that if the seeker of truth leaves the School, he loses contact with the inspiration of the Ray, and is not capable of becoming connected by himself again.

When the energy cocoon of the disciple is closed, it is difficult for him to establish a metaphysical contact with the School. But if he manages to open it again, he feels the inspiration of the School, the impulse of the Ray, and he will have no doubts about his choice. If not, then he will follow the crowd, considering its view a reference point of the 'right choice'.

The nature of the inner light is mysterious and unfathomable; it is beyond the comprehension of the manifested world. Therefore, whatever explanation we have for this phenomenon, the mind will always be dissatisfied. The nature of the inner light is sacred, it is impossible to explain, and one can only experience it.

If you reside in the sphere of mind, you witness a ceaseless dialogue between different 'selves', which prevents you from experiencing the real Self.

If you realize that you are not your mind, if you can experience that you are a spiritual being, then the path to inner freedom is open to you.

When you have stopped the inner dialogue, you can dip into your inner world and cognise the nature of inner light. You will swim in its rays, enjoying inner freedom.

You will need no intellectual evidence; your own inner experience will be enough. You will have a deep wish to experience this state of bliss again.

* * *

When the inner light illuminates my consciousness I fly on the wings of my soul into the dwelling of pure joy. Immersing in the inner peace I find rest from the worldly commotion around me.

Shifting perception I look with amazement at the changing of my inner states.

Having shifted it to my left side I begin to perceive my future life in the world hereafter.

I once caught sight of how I shall meet the Master after my death, resuming the building of the School which was started during life.

Life in the astral body will continue until the moment of the new incarnation, and then a new flesh and a new astral body will be born. This picture of my future life made my soul peaceful.

The change of the astral body causes the loss of memory of the past incarnation, because the memory of the last incarnation is stored there. It shows that astral and physical bodies depend on each other, and the one is the extension of the other.

When the physical body dies, its astral double remains and continues to live in the eight worlds hereafter. But when the time of incarnation comes, we lose it, receiving a new physical body and a new astral double.

This cycle of incarnation and death repeats itself every time and is called the Wheel of Samsara.

Someone who has found the School during earthly life, has a chance to continue studying there in the world hereafter. There are many different schools in the worlds hereafter and man may join the one or the other.

When one uses the mystical stalking, one will be able to study in several schools, but it is necessary to first master the spiritual practices which are in accordance with the Spirit of Time.

The mystical stalking is most important, because it paves the way for contact with the adepts in the world hereafter, which gives new possibilities. For if man is engaged only in social stalking, it can dissolve his positive potential, dissipate the inner light. It is necessary therefore to build an alchemical laboratory within, which restores the lost radiance.

Long-lasting solitude does not give much perspective and if a man has not mastered the art of communication with other people during his life, he will not learn it after his death. Stalking is a special gift, a secret art to carry the light of the teaching into the world of the amoeba, without breaking its balance, as well as into the world of human beings. Mystical stalking is the ability to communicate with angels.

When you learn to communicate easily with other people during your life, you will be able to communicate with them with the same easiness in the worlds hereafter.

Communication has value only when it happens on the level of essential understanding and subtle romanticism, otherwise it is useless.

A man is an obstinate creature, and he learns slowly, and changes his point of view and convictions even more slowly, so that you need not count on a rapid learning process.

In order to explain the idea of the Path to a neophyte it is necessary, to make many efforts, and to give him as much attention and care as you would give a fragile plant.

It is not simple to find the way to another man's heart, and it is even more complicated to make him enthusiastic about the idea of development.

For he sleeps and the dream of maya is deep.

When I shift my point of perception to the left, I become aware of the world hereafter and my belonging to it. It changes then from a frightening abstraction to the familiar reality that I will have to master again.

Together with the incarnation on earth, man loses his astral double of the former incarnation, which knew the threads of the world hereafter very well. His new double must explore the world hereafter again. The double is born simultaneously with the physical body, of which it is an inseparable copy. The development of the double runs parallel with the development of the physical body. Man has a task to establish a conscious connection and communication with it, and to learn to control the astral double as skilfully as he does with the physical body.

With the help of the astral double we can explore the world hereafter.

It is known that the experiences of an incarnation on earth are still accessible for reflection after the death of the physical body, but those are completely lost with the next birth on earth. Man's personality dissolves into the universal ether, and he will not recollect his previous incarnation. He will be like an empty sheet of paper on which his new personality will be depicted.

If man succeeds to feel about for the point of memories of previous incarnations, then by shifting his perception there he will recollect his past lives.

He will recollect himself and all his reflections through thousands of years and he will understand who he is and the experiences he had in his previous incarnations.

The problem is how to activate the point of perception which is responsible for the memory of incarnations, how to find the key.

If the perception of the person is on the right side of the body, then the meeting with the astral double might be shocking. But if the perception is shifted to the left, the meeting with people from the world hereafter will be natural.

This fact shows the conflict which exists between the subtle and the rough points of support of man.

It is easy in the left-side state of consciousness to communicate with entities of the world hereafter and it is perceived as a natural and painless experience. It gives an opportunity to penetrate into the astral worlds.

Once I walked on the sunny coast of the Baltic Sea. The sand was covered with silver shells. The sun was slowly approaching the horizon and I decided to perform some magical passes near the blue water.

After five minutes I felt that an invisible golden wind filled my soul with radiance and golden pollen. At the same moment I sensed my astral body which shined clearly being covered with this pollen, standing up against the background of the physical body.

I realized that I could easily travel with this astral body in cosmic space, visiting different planets and solar systems. This experience was so explicit and natural that I was staggered for a moment. I felt that I could easily detach myself from my physical body and rush with the speed of thought into the unfathomable deep.

It seemed to me that somewhere in the heaven there is a mysterious city, which fills the space around it with golden radiance.

I sat down on the sand and immersed myself in meditation, fixed my gaze on the sunset and enjoyed the golden vibration of light.

* * *

CIBENCIS: THE ANDROGENIC CHILD IS FED WITH THE VIRGIN'S MILK

This engraving represents the androgenic child born from the Red King and White Queen. The defenceless infant needs vigilant motherly care for his further growth. It is necessary for him, in order to maintain the process of the intensifying of radiant light, to be nourished with the Virgin's Milk – a mysterious light of the Universal Soul. At the same time the Alchemist humbly prays before the icon of our Lord asking for the secret fire, without which the further process of the growth and transmutation of the volatile, and at the same time stable androgen, is impossible.

A neophyte in order to immerse into the unknown depth of himself should create the matter Rebis, which originates from the alliance of the purified Sulphur and glittering Quicksilver. For a successful growth of the two-in-one Rebis, the help of the secret fire is necessary. However, the Virgin's Milk coming from the Mother of God is also indispensable. The energy of the secret fire helps his power to grow, while the golden light opens up the mysteries of the universe for him.

The two-in-one Rebis still can easily dissipate and therefore the experienced Alchemists keep him in a hermetically sealed vessel under their constant watch.

Immersed in my inner world I felt myself a silver light again. It brought me a great relief, for the past days were filled so much with daily routine that I had deeply identified with the body and forgotten about the inner light.

It was still present in my soul, but the dream of maya managed to penetrate into my heart and poisoned it with its illusion.

I stopped controlling the position of the point of my perception, and immediately became imprisoned in matter by my physical point of support. The point of perception was fixed in the physical body, and I began to perceive the physical world as the only reality accessible to me. I could not contact the subtle worlds, the gates of another perception were closed, and I fell into the dream of my physical point of support. I had again reached a deadlock of perception, and the manifested world had entrapped my consciousness.

In this situation the mind does not perceive the spiritual worlds, it just furiously whispers: 'It is all delirium, it is all nonsense'.

My perception narrowed to the 5 senses of the physical body, I lost my intuition and subtle perception.

I became a common inhabitant of the earth, a stupid narrow-minded one. Staring at my reflection in the mirror, I thought: 'Is this material puppet me?'

'No,' an inner voice answered, 'it is not you, it is just a visible part of you. It comes from the worlds hereafter, and you perceive it in the form of body. Your invisible part lives in other dimensions, which you can scarcely imagine. If you commit yourself to the earthly vision, you will always be doomed to failure.'

The reflection in the mirror started to vibrate and became a large threatening size, and it seemed to try to stretch out its arm to me through the mirror. I recoiled abruptly because it felt as if the double tried to drag me into its ghostly world.

I looked closely at my body and touched my face, and then my arm, and with a feeling of terror I realized that it was not me. Immediately I wanted to detach myself from this fellow who ate my supper every evening, slept on my bed and responded to my name.

And though it is obvious that this fellow just imitates me, sometimes he manages to delude me, suggesting that he is me and that I am him.

And when this happens I say over and over again, day and night: 'I am an immortal Spirit.'

* * *

Coming into a meditative state I ask: 'Who am I? Who am I? Who am I?' Going still deeper, I discover that I am a radiant substance and I am entirely filled with inner bliss. Bathing in this bliss I forget the flow of time.

Immersing in the depth of my soul I perceive myself as a conscious light, a kind of immaterial reflective being who can travel in space with ease. A being who can easily enter any physical body and abandon it again.

I feel part of a fairy tale which I entered into because of my sudden awakening.

I begin to realize that I am a thinking spirit, who dwells wherever he wishes.

The only barrier is that I fell asleep because I identified with my body of this incarnation.

Nevertheless my daily meditations give me an opportunity to awaken from this long sleep and to again feel perfect inner freedom.

I clearly realize now that I am an immaterial substance, equipped with the power of reasoning, which needs awakening and strives for inner freedom.

I am not interested in regarding myself as this transient body and to think that I will die together with it.

I know now that I am a spiritual being which has incarnated on this earth to open up its Highest Self.

I am absolutely convinced now that I am an immaterial reflective spirit which longs for his eternal fatherland.

I am a spirit confined to matter, which wishes to be no longer enslaved by it.

I am a spirit wishing to be kindled with its own light and to return to the worlds where I came from.

I am immaterial and immortal, I want to liberate myself forever from the chains of matter.

I am the one who wants to no longer merge with the body and its deeds. I am the spark of the Absolute aspiring to the summits of the spirit.

I can wander eternally in the universe, regardless of space and time.

* * *

Thoughts come and go and the soul, who is always there, must track their traces. I immersed myself in meditation early in the morning, trying to recognize myself as a spiritual being separate from the physical body, which is a key-point of self-observation. I realized that dreams intensify my identification with the body, though one might logically suppose that it would be weakened, because in our dreams we are free from our physical body.

But my experience is that in dreams I move away from my essence, and therefore through meditation I must immerse in myself every morning, trying to recollect who I am and what is the purpose of my incarnation. When in the morning I remember myself as a golden light, then all day long I feel its radiance. If not, then the day passes under the pressure of the physical body and it's problems, and the pragmatic mind repeats to me:

'You are just your body, and the world in which it lives is the only reality.'

'But the soul belongs to the divine spheres,' I object.

'Look around, you will find neither God nor his angels,' the mind sneers sceptically.

Then, immersing in myself, I disengage from the transient body, and the mind is forced to acknowledge it.

At such moments I feel myself a spiritual being, dressed in a physical shell, trying to find the secret door between the worlds, longing to enter another reality. For me it is not interesting to reside in the manifested world. I endlessly investigate worlds behind the curtain, shifting my perception, trying to penetrate the mystery of fairy tales, into the reality behind the mirror.

Sometimes I become a volatile part of infinity, perceiving myself as an immeasurable space. Then I swim in the coolness of the reflected radiance of the sun, in an immeasurable void of invisible worlds, smiling at an eternal spring.

The man of metamorphosis considers his body as a dress-suit, to visit the ball of life, and he leaves it with the same ease, immersing himself into the radiance of the soul, rejoicing in her divine nature. With the ease of air he disperses himself through the whole universe, and turns into radiant light, dissolving in its immense vastness, drowning in bliss. Each of us can become a man of metamorphosis.

The time spent in unravelling the mystery of man is never wasted. An attempt to enter one's own inner world, beyond the secret door behind which the mysterious sphinx hides, is an exciting adventure in the labyrinth of uncertainty.

* * *

ALBERTUS MAGNUS

This engraving represents an alchemist dressed in ritual garments, holding the stuff
in his left hand, symbol of the spiritual power that he found in the process of obtaining the Philosophers Stone. He points with his right hand to the divine androgen
which unites the pure Sulphur – the male principle of the spirit, and pure mercury
– the volatile female principle aspiring to Anima Mundi. These two principles in the
Androgen ceased their eternal struggle and aspired towards the perfection. By this
time the silver light manifests itself in the seeker of God, which can serve as the
lodestar on the long and arduous Path of Reintegration.

If this light dims in the soul, it means that the seeker moves away from the Path; if
the light becomes brighter, it means that he goes in the right direction.

MEDITATION 20: THE LIGHT OF THE HIGHEST SELF

The highest task of man is to search for his lost Divine nature, to search for his own sacred depth, which belongs to the Absolute Origin of all Origins.

The light of the Highest Self is a radiant spark of the Absolute which shines in the darkness of the fallen worlds.

The light of the inner sun has a mysterious nature and it is sacred and incomprehensible to the daily consciousness. It shines from a mysterious height, and we have to discover it by immersing in the depths of ourselves.

The invisible light of the Highest Self is present deep within us, as the divine lodestar. A person who follows it will never lose his way and will never leave the path leading to reintegration. But it is not an easy path, and in order to follow it a continuous inner effort is indispensable.

When the golden disc of the invisible sun flames up in your heart, you may be certain that the Highest Self has descended into the physical body.

The Highest Self gives us the right to enter the spiritual worlds, which exist on a much higher level than the manifested world of matter.

Immersing myself in a mysterious inner world, I dive into the bliss of inner light, its radiance in my heart helps me to follow the Path without becoming a victim of many temptations of the outer world.

Immersing in myself I see past incarnations, which are just a pale reflection of the intentions of the Highest Self, they are only his shadows.

I try to penetrate into the mystery of myself in order to comprehend: ' Who am I?'

Meditating on the creation I discover that the Absolute is the only reality, and that the manifested worlds are no more than His reflections. I dwell in one of these worlds, but I have to return home, to the spiritual world I once left. When I entered the worlds of reflection of the Absolute, I lost my memory and remembered nothing of my past. I am longing to return home, to that real world which is my spiritual homeland.

When I realize that I lost all memories of the past, I am shattered. I understand that I do not know at all who I am, I have to recall myself and find my friends with whom I wandered in the reflected worlds.

Who am I, and where must I go?

I see that there is a lot of work waiting: the restoration of my memory. I have an incessant wish to return to that world where I came from, to return to that magic city where I dwelled before. With a clear goal now, to return to the radiant world, I realize how tired I am of wandering in the reflected worlds. I do not remember how many centuries I spent in the worlds of reflection, on the various planets of our universe.

Again, out of all these wanderings I come to a very important conclusion that the best thing for me to do is to return to the heavenly dwelling, which I left long ago.

Now it is necessary to answer the following question: How should I do it?

My life on earth is not really mine; because the larger part is the life of my body, although I do my best to transform it into the life of my essence. When I forget that I am a spirit and perceive myself as a physical body, I lose my inner radiance and my mind immediately begins to insinuate: 'There is no light within you.'

Knowing by now the tricks of perception I shift my consciousness to a point, where my mind gains access to the perception of the astral body, and then I start to perceive the world hereafter.

It means that it is not only the material nature of the mind that matters, but also the kind of information that the mind has to deal with. If the mind receives information from the astral body, it includes this information into its operating area saying to us that the astral world exists. If the mind receives information only from the physical body it tells us that only a physical world exists. So it is not mind itself that we deal with, but with what it perceives. Mind is able to perceive the world not only by means of a physical point of support but by means of an astral one as well. We have to learn to discriminate and master the perception of both bodies.

Man can say that the art of remembering himself is learning the skill of directing his perception. If I do not know how to do it, then remembering myself remains a mental exercise, or is limited to the observation of the physical body. In the last case this idea really comes from the spheres of spirit and essence to the physical level, losing its metaphysical nature. Therefore the practice of remembering oneself should start with the handling of one's own perception. Only when one has learned to shift perception to the astral body, does the astral plane become accessible to our feelings and sensations.

Reasoning by the logic of the shifting of perception, we come to the following conclusion: man in order to become aware of his own essence, has to shift perception to a certain point of the *energy cocoon*, and then he will perceive the radiance of the awakened essence. Only then can man remember himself, which means his own essence, and he will not confuse it with the astral or the physical body. Another question is how to shift the point of perception to those positions on the *energy cocoon*, from which we can become aware of ourselves as a luminous being and perceive the world hereafter? And the last question is: How can man perceive his own three-fold nature and the spiritual world beyond the boundaries of the manifested Universe?

* * *

Once I had to perform Tensegrity exercises in a room where I felt a spirit of hatred and alienation, and a cold spirit penetrated me. I lost the sensation of my radiant essence and became arrogant and scornful towards my friends, feeling alienated and separated from them.

I hoped that the cold would dissolve in the warmth of my heart after a night of sleep, but in the morning the state of alienation became even stronger.

The inner light was extinguished and a gloomy irritation overflowed me. I immersed myself in meditation, trying to kindle the inner light, but all was in vain, the perception had shifted into the material world and become firmly fixed there. I couldn't imagine that just yesterday I felt a radiant being. I became identified with matter so deeply, that any idea of spiritual growth seemed to be a strange fantasy. For several hours I tried unsuccessfully to get out of this state, but in the second half of the day the inner light started to glimmer faintly in my soul. Gradually the radiance of inner light illumined my soul, and again I sensed myself as light, as an inextinguishable spark of the Absolute.

Having shifted my perception and being separated from my body, I felt the breath of freedom. I realized that the highest part of my soul has a direct link with the Master and is able to unite with him in the space of inner radiance. In the manifested worlds I am separated from him by a diversity of forms, which makes us feel like separate beings. But we are one in the depth of our soul, in the radiance of the inner light. And when I have ill feelings towards him, I soon fall into the space of hell.

But if I totally accept the Master, becoming one with his spirit, then I am again in the sphere of inner radiance. It is not good to have ill feelings towards him, because he is the light in the darkness in this world. If I revolt against him, I revolt against my own Highest Self.

When the Master approaches me an invisible door to the highest worlds opens, and the light in my soul flames up with incredible intensity. He is the secret mediator of an invisible power, who stimulates the cognising of the Highest Self. Any opposition towards him, disguised even as innocent resentment, shuts off the passage to the highest worlds. If I am separated from him I am separated from my Highest Self as well. The only thing I can do is to follow him always and everywhere.

Once I managed to overcome the wall of alienation and entered his radiance. I realized that I am a thinking spirit, a spiritual being who in the past dwelled in the highest worlds. This light was flaming up with every new second, overflowing my whole being. My soul started to shine like an inextinguishable lamp in the night. I became aware of myself as a radiant being without a visible form.

I am a thinking spirit, floating easily in an invisible space, and feeling a subtle sorrow about his imprisonment in the world of forms in the astral and physical universes. I wander as a prisoner through the manifested cosmos, changing bodies and forms. I often lose clarity of consciousness, besotted by the hypnosis of maya, and flowing together with forms in which I incarnate.

I am a radiant spirit, returning to his spiritual homeland, the source of primordial light. I regret that I forget so often who I am, losing the awareness of my essential Self.

In such moments I become part of matter, a physical body with an astral double attached to it, of which I am hardly aware.

But if I manage to recall myself, I become a radiant spirit wandering beyond space and time in the manifested universe. It gives me the sensation of great freedom and a remembrance of my spiritual homeland.

* * *

DEMOCRITUS

The engraving represents the alchemist pointing to the lily-white alchemical Venus. She was born under the light of the stars in her divine glory, after the Androgen has passed through the stages Nigredo and Albedo.

The Nigredo signifies the descending of the Androgen into the lower spheres of the soul and passing under the guidance of the stalker the labyrinth of Minotaurus. The Androgen undergoes a meeting with his own death, after which all impurity hidden in the depth of his soul burns out, and his body becomes covered with the dark taint. The Androgen, in order to wash away these dark impurities, should undergo the stage Albedo, where all the dead things will be removed from his soul, and she will be washed in pure heavenly waters. Young Venus touches the heavenly Anima Mundi with the wings of her soul and embraced by her, immerses in the cognition of the mysteries of the being.

Today I got up at dawn. This is the best time for meditation. The city still sleeps and the restless thoughts of people hurrying to their jobs do not disturb my consciousness. I soon immersed myself in my meditation, and proceeded with the investigation of the phenomenon of consciousness.

I am pure consciousness; I am a bright light fallen into the manifested world.

I am a radiant consciousness dressed in different forms.

I am pure light which entered the world of forms.

I am pure light installed in a physical body.

I am pure light fallen into the world of matter.

I am pure light which has forgotten its divine origin.

I am pure light clothed in different physical shells.

I am pure light darkened by matter.

I am pure light which went down into the worlds of matter

I am pure light imprisoned by physical perception.

I am pure light which has forgotten about its radiant nature.

I am pure light which has forgotten its spiritual fatherland.

I am pure light hidden under the cover of maya.

I happened to be there where the consciousness becomes clouded soon and the memory of our light origin disappears.

I became identified with a false perception of myself as one of the forms of maya.

'You and I are one,' the Master says to me. 'As pure light we fell into the manifested world and appeared there in different forms, though in eternity we remain particles of the primordial light, created by the Divine Consciousness. I shall never lose you, because we belong to one and the same radiance. Being transformed into light I can find you everywhere, and fly to you through space and time, and become you, as you become me. But maybe, I shall not return and remain there, while you remain here.'

'I am pure light and I shall return into the worlds of radiant spirit.'
'I am pure light shining in the night of the fallen world.'
'I am a primordial light, clothed in the diverse forms of the manifested worlds.'
'I am pure light which is aware of its sacred nature.'
'I am a bodiless spirit shining with golden light in the depths of the manifested universe.'
'I am pure light which descended into the bosom of matter and became identified with it.'
'In order to reunite with you I shall return to my radiance, and on the wings of a flash I will cover years and distances.'

* * *

Going deeper in meditation I realize that I am a spiritual being sheathed in a material shell.

A far-away dawn starts to glitter within me and my heart feels unspeakable bliss.

I am a radiant spark of the Absolute and He is my true Father.

I am an immortal spark of the Absolute and He has commanded me to come to Him and to recognize Him within my heart.

I am an all-living spark of the Absolute and He obliged me to strive for the golden radiance of the soul.

I am an inextinguishable spark of the Absolute and He commanded me to follow His voice, which resounds in my heart from time to time.

I am an immortal spark of the Absolute and He commanded me to follow His directions, which appear in my consciousness.

I am a radiant spark of the Absolute Origin of all Origins and I feel His radiance on my forehead.

I am an eternal spark of the Absolute and I hear His distant voice calling for my return into the Divine bosom, like a lighthouse of eternity shining in the darkness of the world.

I am a starry spark of the Absolute and His call resounds in my consciousness.

I am a thinking spark of the Absolute Origin of all Origins, which has awakened from the sleep of the world hypnosis and aspires towards a lost unity.

I am a radiant spark of the Absolute; I desire to unite with my Father and to co-create with Him consciously and joyfully.

I am an inextinguishable spark of the Absolute Origin of all Origins, which desires to become united with his grace, desiring to satiate its soul with heavenly love.

I am a radiant spark of the Absolute which wishes to return into the bosom of its Father.

I am a spark of the Absolute Origin of all Origins, desiring to glow with inner light, immersing in indescribable bliss.

I am a solar spark of the Absolute and I shall not forget my Father, I remember the vow that I made to Him: to return from the abyss of the fall into the worlds of the sacred Spirit.

* * *

1. Experiencing the cosmic space.

Lie down on your back and relax your body. Try to feel that your body, beginning with arms and legs, becomes warm. You should relax until you lose the sensation of the physical body.

Imagine then that your head becomes more and more cold. When the head has become completely cold your should leave your body through the crown of the head. Then you can experience an astral flight in the cosmos.

2. Meditation on the inner light.

Sit down in a meditation posture with your legs crossed. Straighten your spine and relax your body. Inhale the energy through the so called *point of death* which is situated at a distance of two fingers width below the navel. Move energy still inhaling through an energy channel to the spine and then move it further through the central channel of the spine to the crown of the head.

While exhaling partly move energy downwards along the backside of the spinal column to the point which is situated between the shoulder blades. Holding your breath concentrate at the same time on the point of inner light which is situated outside the body at the distance of couple of centimetres from the point where have brought the energy.

Still holding your breath and concentrating on the point of inner light, turn your head rhythmically from left to right and back in the sector of approximately 30 degrees. Keep your mouth slightly open so that the rest of the air in your lungs could escape.

Then repeat the entire cycle all over again. You should constantly concentrate on the point of inner light until you feel that there is some light starts dawning/glimmering in your soul.

This exercise should be performed every day at least for half an hour.

It's important, however, to distinguish the quality of the light. There can be a cold light, of a luciferic kind; and there can be warm, cordial kind of light. There can also be a kind of cool light. It is essential is not to fall into the cold light because then the person comes under the influence of the *cold current*.

3. Beyond the physical body experience.

It's possible to leave the physical body with the help of the technique which is similar to the technique of the meditation on the inner light. The difference is that while exhaling you should move the energy from the crown of the head to the point which is situated outside of the body on the distance of couple centimetres from the middle of the cervical part of the spine.

INTERVIEWS WITH THE MASTER

Once while travelling in the East, Pjotr Demijanovich Ouspensky met a Zen Patriarch and interviewed him in order to collect material for his book.

He asked:

'Could you, Sir, clarify the idea of the Zen path?'

The Patriarch looked closely into the eyes of Ouspensky, and asked in return:

'Do you know who you are?'

'A man,' Ouspensky answered astonished

'That is obvious, but who are you?'

'The author,' Ouspensky answered again.

'I understand, but who are you really?'

'I am the disciple of the well-known Mister Gurdjieff,' Ouspensky had an idea of how to answer.

'I understand this as well, but who are you, yourself?' Patriarch Zen asked again.

'I am the man who always remembers himself,' Ouspensky answered confused.

'And which self do you remember?' Patriarch Zen pressed him with this question.

'Stop trying to mislead me,' Ouspensky answered chilly.

'Which of your selves am I trying to mislead?' Patriarch Zen asked with curiosity.

Ouspensky turned slightly scarlet.

'If you stop writing about things you have not experienced, then I am prepared to welcome you as a disciple,' the Patriarch answered in a serious manner and left Ouspensky in a gloomy state of mind.

Mister Gurdjieff often teased those who regarded him as his physical shelter, for he saw himself as the spirit incarnated in the body.

Pjotr Demijanovich Ouspensky who considered himself a disciple of Gurdjieff, wrote books in which he persuaded people to remember themselves. He even gave it a name: 'Work on oneself,' and he stated that his teaching, 'The Fourth Way', leads to liberation even without the help of the spiritual master.

Did he himself understand the ideas he described so attractively? How did he perceive himself? Perhaps as that very body that wrote the book In Search of the Miraculous? Did he really know which self he ought to remember?

His essence could not recollect herself, being entrapped by the body. That is the reason why Ouspensky, despite all attempts, did not find his own spirit. It is known that just before his death he repented, realizing that he was not a Master and that his system does not lead to possibilities for man to cognise himself.

Man has fallen into the mental trap of the physical and the astral body, which are the points of support in the physical and astral world.

These have their own personalities, emotions and experiences, which man takes as his essential consciousness.

Most people fall into this trap and often mistake themselves for these puppets, and this keeps people in delusion.

Emotion and passion belongs to the material and astral points of support, and not to the essential Self of man. But these points of support have consumed the attention of man to such an extent that he cannot break away from their embrace and realize his true Self.

'Who are you?' The Master asks.

It is difficult to answer this question being trapped in bodies, in the lowest part of man's self. The Master's question arises from the real Self, but the disciple answers from his illusory self, on behalf of his bodies. The Master tests the disciple, for the Master dwells deeper within himself than the person he questions.

The total identification of the real Self with the bodies, is called the hypnotic sleep (dream) of maya, from which one cannot wake up and realize that he is an imperishable spirit. Even death cannot save him from this illusory dream of maya.

Death frees man only from the physical body, the point of support in the worlds of matter, but one immediately falls into the trap of the perception of the astral body, which does not bring him one step closer to his Highest Self.

The Highest Self is a source of primordial light, which was granted to us by the Absolute.

A man in his essence is beyond any expression a radiant spark of the Absolute; he is part of Him, having inherited the living nature of the Creator Himself. And the task of man is to awaken, to recollect his divine primacy. The light of the divine nature of man is buried under a thick layer of bodies that he has found as a result of a cosmic catastrophe - the fall of our universe into the worlds of matter.

* * *

HERMES: THE SECRET FIRE

The patriarch of the Art of Alchemy, fabulous Hermes Trismegistus, points with his left hand to the alliance of the sun and the moon. This alliance gives birth to the secret fire, which makes the alchemical Gold out of the alchemical Venus – the passing of Venus through the Rubedo phase of the Work. The perfect alchemical agent can be obtained only through the union of two fires.

It becomes at a later stage cosmic gold – the Philosophers Stone

Once in the afternoon I came to see the Teacher, and humbly prostrated before him I asked:
'Could you tell me, honourable Master, about the great Path of Ascension?'
'Do you know to whom you are talking?' He asked suddenly.
'Yes, I know you for so many years.'
'Are you sure that it is the real me?'
'I am certain of it, you are not a twin are you?'
'This is, however, not me, this is something else, he commented in an aloof manner.'
'I know, you like teasing.'
'It is a pity that you cannot see the real me.'
'Whom do I see then?'
'You see the body, but not the real me.'
'I have always seen you in this way,' I insisted.
'How can I tell you about the Path, if you are not able to see me behind this screen of the body?'
'What should I do then?'
'Look behind the visible body.'
'What should I see then?'
'You will see my real Self.'
'It sounds like some sort of delirium,' I became suddenly angry.
'I agree, this is a delirium of your perception,' he answered and laughed. 'You trust your mind, which is in an illusion.'
'What is this illusion?'
'If I would compare the truth to an elephant, you see only its trunk.'
'In this case I see only your trunk, isn't it?' I laughed. 'And where is the elephant himself?'
'He is also present, but you do not see him.'
'What is this that I see?' I woke up.

'You see only the trunk of the essence of things,' he said, 'you are the slave of the fixed perception. Shift your perception into another place, and the world will instantly become transformed.'

'Do you mean that as long as I do not change my perception I will not understand you?'

'You will not understand the idea of path as well,' he smiled. 'The way you understand the Path now is opposite to what I mean.'

'You say that I am hopeless.'

'Here you have the first step on the Path: learn to shift your perception into the world behind the mirror.

Your mind is focused on matter, and it will never see the flight of the spirit.'

He thus sketched before me an invisible hieroglyph that I could not decipher.

* * *

I came to visit the Master after my long unsuccessful meditations.
He was sitting silently beside the fire.
I asked him feeling disappointed:
'Why do you insist on the necessity to meditate daily on inner light?
I would like to hear the reason why.'
'An intellectual cognition of the doctrine of inner light is useful only
if you give lectures on this subject. Remember that if you do not
meditate daily, the golden radiance of your soul may extinguish.'
'Notwithstanding this statement, I would first like to be convinced
of the necessity of this practice,' I insisted.
'You suggest that I should meet your unenlightened mind,' the Mas-
ter commented, 'but I would like you to conquer its scepticisms.'
'You are afraid to clash with the logic of my mind,' I commented
suspiciously.
'It is logic of narrow perception,' he commented pityingly.
'You just are not able to help me.'
'I point to the Path, but it is you who should walk on it.'
'However before I start, you should prove to me that I am not wast-
ing my time.'
'Are you sure that you are not wasting it already?'
'Time is money,' I smiled.
'I do not see that you have either at your disposal.'
'I still have time, because I am young.'
'The young donkey will become an old donkey,' he said grinning,
'and still he will think that the time spent on the opening up of the
divine nature was wasted.'
'I have to be certain about the positive result,' I said indignantly.
'I see you do not like risks!'
'I do not like incalculable risks,' I answered irritated.

'Whenever I point to the Path it will always challenge your selfish-ness, he commented. Nevertheless you will always be a radiant spark of the Absolute.'

* * *

After several days I became aware of my insignificance and turned to the Master asking for his help again.

'What is the Path?' I asked him.

'One may call the Path the art of entering through a door without a door.'

'What is that?' I asked astonished.

'It is a door without a door.'

'How can I enter if it does not exist in the nature of things,' I asked listening intently.

'It does not exist in the nature of your mind,' he answered grinning.

'You answered but you said nothing,' I commented feeling a slight displeasure.

'I said nothing to your mind, but I transmitted something to your Self.'

'Is there any difference between me, to whom you transmitted something, and my mind that you try to perplex?'

'The one who perceives is you, and the one who asks is the mind.'

'However I do not see any difference between my mind and me.'

'That is the reason why you are in a delusion,' he answered with authority.

'Do you dare to state that I am something other than my mind?'

'That is it,' he said. 'The mind questions, while your true self perceives.'

'It happens simultaneously in me,' I answered confused.

'You stick to your mind as a burdock. Stop it, and then the right thing will happen to you.'

'I can stop a cab, an oscillating lamp beneath the ceiling, but how can I stop the mind if it is not to be found. I am becoming irritated with this senseless talk.'

'I tell about the Path while you talk about nothing,' he said and looked at me piercingly.

I wanted to go on with the argument, but his estranged glance stopped me. There were no questions in my head anymore, as if they had evaporated. I felt in my pocket and took out a notebook in which I stored my questions. When I opened it he gave me such a wall-eyed look, that the notebook fell out of my hands.

I stood and stared at him not knowing what to do.

He kept silent, and so did I; the situation was taking on an absurd character.

'You try to hypnotize me,' I said, with a feeling of relief and burst out laughing.

'You are one in a thousand idiot,' he commented. 'I stopped your mind but you think it is an honour to start the inner dialogue again.'

'I am the one who is accustomed to having a clear idea of what is going on within me; I do not want to dwell in delusion.'

'You dwell in delusion all the time,' he burst out laughing straight in my face.

'Clear thinking prevents delusion,' I commented chilly.

'Your clear thinking operates with a false perception.'

'How do you know that your perception is genuine?'

'You are the one who comes to me with the questions.'

'It means nothing,' I erupted.

'It says everything,' he declared, 'your spirit calls for help.'

* * *

SENDIGOVIUS: THE MAGICAL GARDEN WITH SOLAR AND LUNAR TREES

This engraving represents the Alchemist who has successfully accomplished both Minor and Great Work, which is symbolized by the trees with solar and lunar fruits. Minor Work has the name Agrioppea and its final outcome is the finding of the Lunar Philosopher's Stone, which is capable of transforming all common metals into silver. The Alchemist who has reached this level of transmutation finds himself on the heights of the universal soul; he is bathed in the pearl effulgence of the stars; he is immersed in the world of bliss, soaring to the universal wisdom, to the agate enchantment of countless moons.

The Great Work has the name Chrisoppea and results in the finding of the Solar Philosopher's Stone, capable of transforming all the common metals into gold. When this happens the Universal Spirit takes such a soul on its wings, and elevates her to the House of the Great Sun where on the border of infinity, the mystery of the merging of the awakened soul with the Absolute Origin of all Origins takes place.

I gently entered the house of the great Teacher of the Spirit, and bowed before the Orient Sun and asked him reverently:

'What is the base of perfection on the Path'?

'The awareness of the pure inner nature of the Highest Self of man, which is not born and does not die. The Highest Self of man is primarily perfect and integral, and its pure radiance is the main teacher,' he answered.

'How do you know that the Highest Self is pure in its nature?' I asked with interest.

'I know from my own experiences. The Highest Self shines like a sun within the soul, dwelling there in its perfection and integrity. Though it is boundless, the clouds of the personality always darken it; therefore we do not perceive its primordial light. The light of our essence is imperishable, the mist of passions and false thoughts only obstructs it. If one can clear it, and keep one's essence in purity, then the false thinking does not appear. And then the sun of the Highest Self will manifest itself naturally.'

'How do you know that the Highest Self was never born and will never die?' I asked listening intently.

'Tradition states so. The solar nature of the Highest Self did not appear and will not vanish, and it is pure in itself. The solar nature of the Highest Self exists alone and was never born, it has no connection with the cause-and-effect conditioning. All people without exception are endowed with the solar nature. And though their names and souls are different, their highest selves are perfectly the same and subjected to neither birth nor death.'

'Why do you call the solar nature of the Highest Self the main teacher?' I asked, becoming interested.

'The solar nature of the Highest Self exists naturally, on its own, and does not come to us from outside. There is nothing in the world so intimately close to us as the light bearing nature of the Highest Self.

Acknowledging its solar nature can lead you to enlightenment. The erring forget this and find the lower forms of existence, and for that reason the enlightened consider their solar origin as the teacher,' he said, and after a rigorous look at me continued:

'All the enlightened ones acknowledge their Highest Self, which is the source of primordial light. False thinking is not present in them, and the thought of the existence of the Highest Self does not leave them, they dwell in the radiance of the primordial light in co-creation with the Absolute. Many people are deluded about the essence of their true nature and they do not acknowledge the primordial light of essence. They come again and again into the wheel of incarnation, overwhelmed by the feelings of appealing and repelling, their light-bearing origin darkens and they forget about their divine origin. Mankind drowns in the births and deaths of the manifested world and cannot reach liberation.'

'Why is it that only a few reach spiritual liberation and the others reside in delusion?' I asked with interest.

'Awakening is the acknowledgement of one's light -bearing nature. Delusion is the loss of the radiant nature of the essence. In order not to lose our light-bearing nature, it is necessary to perpetually concentrate on the primordial light of man's own essence. Then the consciousness is not darkened, and inner liberation will be reached naturally and spontaneously. The most important aspect of the teaching is the concentration on one's own light-bearing essence, which gives the inner the opportunity sun to shine in its primary purity. The concentration on the inner sun opens the main gates to the Path.'

'Is it possible to reach enlightenment during one single life?'

'If you wish to reach enlightenment during one single life, then the only worthwhile thing to do is to listen to the radiance of the inner sun. Concentration on the inner sun opens the main gates to the Path. All human beings are endowed with the Highest Self, and this is primarily pure and like a clouded sun. Nevertheless if man con-

centrates on the inner radiance of the Highest Self, false thinking, like clouds, disappear, and the inner sun manifests itself.'
'Is it worthwhile to gather knowledge based on bodily sensations, which lead to death and reincarnation? I asked interested.'
'Our soul is like a mirror, if you wipe off the dust the inner sun will flame up. Unenlightened consciousness cannot teach us anything, its knowledge is doomed to become useless. When you have opened up the inner light, this will turn into a radiant sun with time and will be a genuine education. I showed you a great chariot, filled with jewels and brilliant pearls. But you do not take it and use it for your own benefit. Poor little souls that we are, we are not aware of our inner nature.'
'Do not search for truth outside yourself, it will throw you into the chain of death and reincarnation. Keep the radiance of the inner light in your soul, in all her actions. For those who have forgotten their own radiant essence, sow the seeds of future suffering, and cannot liberate themselves from the chain of birth and reincarnation. Do not allow yourself to fritter your time dissipating your energies.'
'When you start your meditations, be seated correctly, close your eyes and keep your lips together. Look straight in front of you, directing your attention to a far distance and imagine the sun, concentrate on it, hear it. Keep this image constantly, without interruption, and harmonize your breathing with it. People who have a consciousness from which darkness flows, cannot become free of the great disease of death and reincarnation. But those who do not know about the direct Path deserve even more pity, because they drown vainly in the depths of the sea of suffering and reincarnation.'
'Neither teaching nor a spiritual master is able to help those who do not wish to strive sincerely for enlightenment. Man should cognize his inner light and cross over to the other side of existence. Gods cannot take him there by their will. We drown in the sea of suffering only because we do not sincerely long for enlightenment.' 'You

could receive these instructions in your present incarnation. They are clear, try to understand what they mean, understand the necessity of concentration on inner light, for this is a direct path.'

'You may be sincere in your wish to become an enlightened being, and if you engage in this practice you will be granted immeasurable bliss. But if your consciousness is darkened and vain you may become addicted to secular manners and seek fame and profit. Then you will undergo all sorts of misfortunes after your death. Therefore be zealous in your practice. Some are successful if they wear simple clothes, eat simple food and have a clear understanding of the principles of the opening up of inner light.'

'But erring worldly people do not strive for inner light, and because of their unenlightened consciousness suffer great torments. They gain earthly wealth, hoping to reach liberation, but this will only result in the spell of the circle of incarnation. Be diligent in your practice and don't become proud. Only a few who have heard these instructions can realize them. Let the inner sun shine in its purity without being darkened by the mist of earthly feelings. Some of the practicing neophytes cannot manage the methods of concentration and the controlling of their energy, and will therefore not be able to open up the inner light.'

'Sit down in the meditation posture, let your body relax, calm down your mind and shut out any thought. Harmonize your breathing and concentrate your attention in such a way that it is neither outside nor within you. Do it diligently and attentively. Contemplate your own energy quietly and concentrate so that you can experience its continuous water-like flow. Having become aware of your energy, start the practice of inner light quietly and attentively, until the inner light flames up within you. You will succeed in the practice of the direct path, when you have learned how to control your unbalanced energy. Let the golden sun shine in its purity without being clouded by earthly feelings.'

* * *

Lightning Source UK Ltd.
Milton Keynes UK
UKHW010635030420
361283UK00001B/14